BEYOND

SURFACE

PERCEPTION

UNLOCKING THE SECRETS TO UNDERSTANDING OTHERS AND BEING UNDERSTOOD

NICK, A PETERSON

INTRODUCTION

Amidst the pervasive presence of social networks and digital interfaces, authentic human connection frequently eludes recognition, mired in transient interactions and superficial facades. Beyond Surface Perception extends an invitation to undertake a profound expedition one that surpasses the mundane and explores the profound depths of genuine human connections.

ESTABLISHING THE FRAMEWORK: THE CRITICALITY OF AUTHENTIC CONNECTION

A fundamental requirement for human beings is the desire for genuine connection a yearning to be recognized, comprehended, and esteemed in accordance with our true selves. Sincere connection provides spiritual sustenance, providing comfort during periods of hardship and rejoicing during times of happiness. It functions as the foundation of significant interpersonal connections, cultivating compassion, reliance, and shared regard. Given the abundance of distractions in our contemporary society, fostering authentic connections has evolved from a mere aspiration to an essential requirement for our emotional welfare and satisfaction.

THE CONSTRAINTS OF A SURFACE-LEVEL UNDERSTANDING

However, in the midst of the hectic pace of contemporary society, authentic connection frequently evades us, triumphing over the appeal of superficial exchanges and hasty assessments. Surface-level comprehension fails to capture the complexities of human experience, reducing individuals to mere caricatures defined by external appearances or fleeting impressions. Such shallow encounters leave us yearning for deeper connections ones that traverse the boundaries of casual conversation and touch the essence of our shared humanity.

OVERVIEW OF THE BOOK'S PURPOSE AND STRUCTURE

In Beyond Surface Perception, we embark on a multidimensional exploration of human connection, guided by the twin beacons of empathy and understanding. Through a series of reflective inquiries and practical exercises, we unravel the intricacies of human nature, unearthing the layers of emotions, motivations, and beliefs that shape our interactions with others. The book is structured to provide a comprehensive roadmap for deepening connections, from refining empathetic listening skills to navigating emotional terrain and establishing authentic relationships.

As we traverse the chapters, we delve into the art of profound listening, navigating the complexities of emotional expression, and overcoming obstacles to effective communication. Drawing on real-life examples and timeless wisdom, we equip ourselves with the tools and insights necessary to cultivate genuine connections in all aspects of our lives be it professional relationships, personal ties, or community engagements.

Join me on this transformative voyage into the depths of human connection, as we dare to look beyond the surface and embrace the profound beauty of authentic understanding and empathy. Through our collective exploration, may we illumine the path towards a more compassionate and interconnected world.

CHAPTER ONE

UNDERSTANDING THE HUMAN PSYCHE

In the intricate dance of human interaction, beneath the veneer of commonplace encounters lies a vast landscape of complexities that influence our perceptions, behaviors, and relationships. To truly comprehend the dynamics at play, we must embark on a journey into the depths of the human psyche—a journey that incorporates the interplay of emotions, motivations, and beliefs. In this chapter, we delve into the intricacies of human nature, investigating the role of perception in influencing interactions and uncovering the layers that define who we are.

DELVING BENEATH THE SURFACE: THE COMPLEXITY OF HUMAN NATURE

At the core of every individual resides a tapestry of experiences, thoughts, and emotions that weave together to form the essence of their being. Human nature is a multidimensional construct, influenced by a multitude of factors including genetics, upbringing, culture, and personal experiences. From the deepest desires to the darkest anxieties, the human psyche is a labyrinth of complexities yearning to be explored.

To delve beneath the surface is to acknowledge the inherent complexity of human nature—to recognize that each individual is a unique amalgamation of aspirations, desires, and vulnerabilities. It is to embrace the nuances and contradictions that define us, recognizing that the human experience is far from linear or predictable.

By delving beneath the surface, we gain insight into the rich diversity of human experience, cultivating empathy and understanding for the multifarious ways in which individuals navigate the complexities of life. Through empathy, we reconcile the distance between ourselves and others, forging connections that transcend the boundaries of superficiality.

THE ROLE OF PERCEPTION IN SHAPING INTERACTIONS

Perception functions as the lens through which we interpret the world around us, shaping our interactions and influencing our relationships. Yet, perception is inherently subjective, colored by our own biases, experiences, and beliefs. What one individual perceives as a threat, another may see as an opportunity; what one person finds amusing, another may find objectionable.

Understanding the function of perception is essential for navigating the intricacies of human interaction. It requires us to recognize that our perception of reality is not necessarily reflective of objective truth, but rather a subjective interpretation influenced by our own unique perspectives. By cultivating awareness of our own biases and actively seeking to understand the perspectives of others, we can cultivate greater empathy and appreciation for the diversity of human experience.

Moreover, perception is not only influenced by internal factors but also by external stimuli, including social norms, cultural values, and media portrayals. The images and messages we encounter on a daily basis influence our perceptions of ourselves and others, often perpetuating stereotypes and reinforcing biases. By critically scrutinizing the sources of our perceptions and challenging societal norms, we can work towards establishing a more inclusive and empathetic society.

UNCOVERING THE LAYERS: EMOTIONS, MOTIVATIONS, AND BELIEFS

Emotions, motivations, and beliefs are the building elements of the human psyche, propelling our thoughts, actions, and interactions with others. Emotions serve as the basic material of human experience, providing us with valuable insight into our innermost desires and anxieties. From the pleasure of a shared chuckle to the sorrow of a loss, emotions color our interactions, imbuing them with depth and meaning.

Motivations, on the other hand, fuel our actions and influence our behavior, molding the choices we make and the paths we pursue. Whether driven by a desire for success, a longing for connection, or a quest for self-fulfillment, our motivations provide insight into our innermost desires and aspirations.

Beliefs, meanwhile, serve as the framework through which we interpret the world, shaping our perceptions and influencing our attitudes and behaviors. Whether anchored in religious faith, cultural traditions, or personal values, our beliefs inform our understanding of right and wrong, shaping our interactions with others and steering our moral compass.

By uncovering the layers of emotions, motivations, and beliefs that underlie human behavior, we gain a deeper understanding of ourselves and others, nurturing empathy and compassion for the complexities of the human experience. Through empathy, we forge connections that transcend the superficial, building relationships grounded in mutual understanding and respect.

In the voyage to comprehend the human psyche, we must be willing to delve beneath the surface, to confront the complexities and contradictions that define us as individuals. By embracing the richness of human nature and cultivating empathy for the diverse perspectives that influence our interactions, we can forge deeper connections and create a more compassionate and inclusive world.

CHAPTER TWO

THE FOUNDATIONS OF HUMAN CONNECTION

Human connection is the essence of our existence, shaping our relationships, communities, and societies. In this chapter, we delve into the fundamental aspects that underpin human connection, investigating its definition, evolutionary origins, and the psychological theories that cast light on its intricacies.

DEFINING HUMAN CONNECTION

Human connection encompasses the emotional, psychological, and social bonds that bind individuals together. It transcends sheer proximity or interaction, encompassing a deeper sense of comprehension, empathy, and shared experiences. It is the substance of what it means to be human, motivating our need for companionship, belonging, and intimacy.

At its center, human connection involves mutual recognition and resonance between individuals, nurturing a sense of belonging and acceptance. It incorporates various forms of relationships, including familial connections, friendships, romantic partnerships, and communal ties. From fleeting encounters to enduring connections, human connection influences our identities, experiences, and well-being.

THE EVOLUTIONARY BASIS OF CONNECTION

The foundations of human connection can be traced back to our evolutionary history, influenced by the adaptive pressures of survival and reproduction. As social creatures, our ancestors relied on cooperation, communication, and group cohesion to navigate their environments and secure resources. This necessitated the development of social bonds and affiliative behaviors that facilitated collaboration and mutual support.

Evolutionary psychologists propose that human connection performed several essential functions throughout our evolutionary past. Firstly, it enhanced our possibilities of survival by fostering cooperation, collective defense, and resource sharing within social organizations.

Secondly, it facilitated mate selection and reproductive success, as individuals formed intimate connections and parental alliances to rear offspring. Lastly, it provided emotional support, solace, and companionship, mitigating against stress, loneliness, and adversity.

From an evolutionary perspective, human connection is not merely a luxury but a fundamental adaptive strategy that has influenced our social nature and relational capacities over millennia.

PSYCHOLOGICAL THEORIES OF CONNECTION

Psychological theories offer insights into the underlying mechanisms and processes that govern human connection, casting light on its cognitive, affective, and behavioral dimensions. Several prominent theories contribute to our comprehension of how individuals form, maintain, and perceive connections with others.

a. Attachment Theory: Developed by John Bowlby and Mary Ainsworth, attachment theory posits that early experiences with caregivers influence our attachment patterns and interpersonal dynamics throughout life. Secure attachment facilitates trust, intimacy, and emotional regulation, while insecure attachment may contribute to difficulties in forming close relationships.

b. Social Exchange Theory: Rooted in economics, social exchange theory posits that individuals engage in relationships based on the perceived costs and benefits involved. It emphasizes the role of reciprocity, equity, and interdependence in shaping relationship dynamics, with individuals striving to maximize rewards and minimize costs over time.

c. Social Identity Theory: Proposed by Henri Tajfel and John Turner, social identity theory highlights the significance of group membership and identity in influencing interpersonal behavior. It suggests that individuals derive a sense of self-concept and belonging from their social groups, leading to in-group partiality, out-group prejudice, and the formation of social bonds based on shared identities.

d. Interpersonal Attraction Theory: Drawing from social psychology, interpersonal attraction theory examines the factors that influence affinity, attraction, and relationship formation between individuals. It considers factors such as physical attractiveness, similarity, proximity, and reciprocity in shaping interpersonal attraction and relationship outcomes.

e. Communication Theories: Various communication theories, including social penetration theory, uncertainty reduction theory, and communication accommodation theory, offer frameworks for understanding how communication processes influence the development and maintenance of interpersonal connections. These theories emphasize the role of self-disclosure, trust, empathy, and nonverbal communication in fostering relational intimacy and understanding.

In summary, psychological theories provide valuable perspectives on the multifaceted nature of human connection, elucidating the cognitive, affective, and relational processes that underlie our interactions with others.

In this chapter, we have investigated the foundational aspects of human connection, including its definition, evolutionary origins, and psychological underpinnings.

By understanding these fundamental principles, we can gain deeper insights into the nature of our relationships and cultivate more meaningful connections with others.

CHAPTER THREE

THE ART OF DEEP LISTENING

In the cacophony of modern life, where voices clamor for attention and distractions abounds, the art of deep listening stands as a beacon of connection—a pathway to understanding, empathy, and genuine engagement. In this chapter, we delve into the transformative power of deep listening, exploring how it cultivates empathetic skills, techniques for active engagement, and strategies for overcoming barriers to effective communication.

A. CULTIVATING EMPATHETIC LISTENING SKILLS

At the heart of deep listening lies empathy—the ability to understand and share the feelings of another. Cultivating empathetic listening skills requires a willingness to suspend judgment, quiet the internal chatter, and truly immerse oneself in the experience of the speaker. It involves tuning into both verbal and nonverbal cues, recognizing the emotions behind the words, and responding with compassion and understanding.

Empathetic listening begins with empathy—an acknowledgment of the inherent worth and dignity of every individual, regardless of their background, beliefs, or experiences. It requires us to set aside our own preconceptions and biases, approaching each interaction with an open mind and a compassionate heart.

Moreover, empathetic listening entails active engagement—a commitment to being fully present and attuned to the needs of the speaker. It involves asking thoughtful questions, paraphrasing the speaker's words to ensure understanding, and reflecting back their emotions to validate their experience.

By cultivating empathetic listening skills, we create a safe and supportive space for individuals to share their thoughts, feelings, and experiences openly, fostering deeper connections and a greater sense of understanding and belonging.

B. TECHNIQUES FOR ACTIVE LISTENING AND GENUINE ENGAGEMENT

Active listening is more than just hearing; it is a dynamic process of fully engaging with the speaker and demonstrating genuine interest and empathy. Techniques for active listening involve a combination of verbal and nonverbal cues, including maintaining eye contact, nodding in agreement, and using affirmative phrases such as "I understand" or "Tell me more."

One effective technique for active listening is reflective listening, where the listener paraphrases the speaker's words to demonstrate understanding and validate their experience. This not only ensures clarity but also communicates empathy and respect for the speaker's perspective.

Another technique is empathetic mirroring, where the listener reflects back the speaker's emotions to validate their experience and demonstrate understanding. For example, if the speaker expresses frustration, the listener might say, "It sounds like you're feeling frustrated. Is that right?"

Genuine engagement also involves asking open-ended questions to encourage the speaker to share more about their thoughts, feelings, and experiences. This demonstrates a sincere interest in the speaker's perspective and fosters deeper connections and understanding.

By practicing techniques for active listening and genuine engagement, we create an environment where individuals feel valued, heard, and understood, fostering deeper connections and more meaningful relationships.

C. OVERCOMING BARRIERS TO EFFECTIVE COMMUNICATION

Despite our best intentions, barriers to effective communication can arise, hindering our ability to truly listen and connect with others. These barriers may be internal, such as distractions, biases, or preconceived notions, or external, such as environmental noise or cultural differences.

One common barrier to effective communication is the tendency to interrupt or prematurely offer solutions.

This can derail the conversation and make the speaker feel invalidated or unheard. Instead, it is important to practice patience and allow the speaker to fully express themselves before offering input or advice.

Another barrier is the tendency to engage in selective listening, where we only pay attention to information that confirms our existing beliefs or biases. To overcome this barrier, it is important to approach each interaction with an open mind and a willingness to consider alternative perspectives.

Cultural differences can also pose barriers to effective communication, as individuals from different backgrounds may have different communication styles, norms, and expectations. By being mindful of cultural differences and practicing cultural humility, we can create an inclusive environment where all voices are heard and respected.

Ultimately, overcoming barriers to effective communication requires self-awareness, empathy, and a commitment to fostering understanding and connection. By cultivating empathetic listening skills, practicing techniques for active engagement, and addressing barriers head-on, we can create a more inclusive and compassionate world where every voice is valued and heard.

CHAPTER FOUR

NAVIGATING EMOTIONAL TERRAIN

Emotions are the compass of the human experience, guiding our thoughts, actions, and interactions with others. In this chapter, we embark on a journey into the complex terrain of emotions, examining how to recognize and validate them, manage emotional responses in ourselves and others, and develop emotional resilience and empathy along the way.

RECOGNIZING AND VALIDATING EMOTIONS

Emotions are the language of the spirit, providing insight into our innermost thoughts, desires, and anxieties. Yet, in a society that often prioritizes rationality over emotionality, we may find ourselves struggling to recognize and validate our own emotions, let alone those of others.

Recognizing and validating emotions begins with self-awareness—a willingness to acknowledge and embrace our own emotional experiences without judgment or criticism. This requires us to tune into our physiological sensations, thoughts, and behaviors, recognizing the subtle signals that indicate the presence of an emotion.

Validation involves acknowledging the legitimacy of our own emotions and those of others, even if they may seem irrational or inconvenient. It is about honoring the inherent value and dignity of every emotional experience, regardless of its intensity or duration.

By recognizing and validating emotions, we create a secure and supportive space for ourselves and others to express their feelings openly, nurturing a greater sense of connection and understanding.

MANAGING EMOTIONAL RESPONSES IN OURSELVES AND OTHERS

Emotional intelligence is the capacity to recognize, comprehend, and manage our own emotions and those of others. It involves being aware of our emotional impulses, regulating our emotional responses, and responding to others with empathy and compassion.

Managing emotional responses begins with self-regulation—a willingness to pause and reflect before reacting impulsively to a situation. This may involve techniques such as deep breathing, mindfulness, or cognitive restructuring to help us obtain perspective and respond more effectively.

Empathetic listening plays a crucial role in managing emotional responses in others, as it enables us to validate their emotions and provide support and understanding. By offering a listening ear and a compassionate presence, we can help individuals navigate their emotions more effectively and find constructive methods to manage.

Conflict resolution skills are also essential for managing emotional responses in ourselves and others, as they enable us to address differences and disagreements with respect and understanding. By practicing active listening, assertive communication, and compromise, we can resolve conflicts peacefully and strengthen relationships in the process.

BUILDING EMOTIONAL RESILIENCE AND EMPATHY

Emotional resilience is the ability to come back from adversity and manage with life's challenges in a healthy and constructive manner.

It involves developing coping strategies, seeking social support, and maintaining a positive outlook in the face of adversity.

Building emotional resilience begins with self-care—a commitment to prioritizing our physical, emotional, and mental well-being. This may entail activities such as exercise, meditation, journaling, or spending time with loved ones to recharge and replenish our energy reserves.

Empathy is the cornerstone of emotional resilience, as it enables us to comprehend and connect with the experiences of others on a deeper level. By practicing empathy, we not only strengthen our relationships but also cultivate a greater sense of compassion and understanding for the human experience.

Cultivating gratitude is another powerful tool for developing emotional resilience, as it helps us concentrate on the positive aspects of our lives and find meaning and purpose in challenging times. By acknowledging the bounties and opportunities that surround us, we can cultivate a greater sense of resilience and well-being.

In conclusion, navigating emotional terrain requires self-awareness, empathy, and resilience. By recognizing and validating emotions, managing emotional responses in ourselves and others, and developing emotional resilience and empathy, we can navigate the complexities of human emotion with grace and compassion, nurturing deeper connections and a greater sense of well-being along the way.

CHAPTER FIVE

BUILDING AUTHENTIC RELATIONSHIPS

In the intricate web of human connections, authentic relationships serve as the bedrock of trust, understanding, and mutual support. In this chapter, we delve into the art of developing authentic relationships, investigating the crucial elements of establishing trust and vulnerability, fostering mutual respect and understanding, and employing strategies for maintaining these connections over time.

ESTABLISHING TRUST AND VULNERABILITY

Trust is the cornerstone of any authentic relationship—it is the foundation upon which mutual respect, empathy, and intimacy are established. However, trust cannot exist in isolation; it requires vulnerability—the willingness to open ourselves up to others, to share our thoughts, feelings, and experiences authentically, and to risk rejection or judgment in the process.

Establishing trust begins with honesty and transparency— being truthful and forthcoming in our interactions with others, even when it may be unsettling or challenging. This requires us to communicate openly and honestly, to acknowledge our errors and shortcomings, and to honor our commitments and promises.

Vulnerability is the key to deepening trust, as it enables us to forge genuine connections with others by sharing our innermost thoughts, anxieties, and aspirations. By embracing vulnerability, we invite others into our lives and create space for intimacy and connection to flourish.

FOSTERING MUTUAL RESPECT AND UNDERSTANDING

Respect is the cornerstone of healthy relationships—it is the recognition of each other's value, dignity, and autonomy. Fostering mutual respect involves honoring each other's boundaries, opinions, and perspectives, and treating each other with kindness, empathy, and compassion.

Understanding is the bridge that connects us to others—it is the ability to see things from their perspective, to empathize with their experiences, and to validate their feelings and emotions. Fostering mutual understanding requires active listening, empathy, and a willingness to suspend judgment and genuinely engage with others.

Empathy plays a crucial role in fostering mutual respect and understanding, as it enables us to interact with others on a deeper level by recognizing and validating their emotions and experiences. By exercising empathy, we can cultivate a greater sense of compassion and understanding for the complexities of the human experience, nurturing deeper connections and stronger relationships in the process.

STRATEGIES FOR MAINTAINING AUTHENTIC CONNECTIONS OVER TIME

Maintaining authentic connections requires effort, commitment, and a willingness to prioritize relationships amidst the busyness of ordinary life. Strategies for sustaining authentic connections over time include:

Regular communication: Stay in touch with friends and loved ones through regular communication, whether it be through phone calls, texts, emails, or in-person visits. Make an effort to check in on how they're doing, share updates about your life, and express appreciation for their presence in your life.

Quality time: Make time for meaningful interactions with friends and loved ones by scheduling regular excursions, activities, or gatherings. Whether it's a dinner engagement, a weekend getaway, or a simple coffee catch-up, prioritize spending quality time together and cultivating your connections.

Openness and honesty: Be open and honest in your communication with others, expressing your thoughts, emotions, and experiences authentically. Foster an environment of trust and vulnerability by being genuine and transparent in your interactions, and encourage others to do the same.

Conflict resolution: Address conflicts and disagreements with respect and understanding, and work together to find constructive solutions. Practice active listening, empathy, and compromise, and be willing to apologize and forgive when necessary. By resolving conflicts peacefully, you can strengthen your relationships and deepen your connections over time.

CHAPTER SIX

OVERCOMING CHALLENGES AND OBSTACLES IN RELATIONSHIP BUILDING

In the voyage of establishing authentic relationships, challenges and obstacles are inevitable. However, it is how we navigate through these obstacles that truly characterizes the strength and resilience of our connections. In this chapter, we will investigate three critical aspects of overcoming challenges and obstacles in relationship building:

Addressing Miscommunication and Misunderstandings

Handling Conflict with Compassion and Empathy

Repairing and Strengthening Relationships Through Adversity

ADDRESSING MISCOMMUNICATION AND MISUNDERSTANDINGS

Miscommunication and misunderstandings can arise from various factors, including differences in communication patterns, cultural contexts, and personal experiences. These disruptions in communication can lead to conflicts and strain relationships if left unaddressed.

To address miscommunication and misunderstandings effectively, it is essential to practice active listening and empathy. This involves sincerely seeking to understand the other person's perspective, acknowledging their emotions and concerns, and validating their experiences. By demonstrating empathy and comprehension, we can create a safe and supportive environment for open and honest communication.

Additionally, clarifying expectations and intentions can help prevent misunderstandings from occurring in the first place. Clearly expressing our thoughts, feelings, and intentions, and seeking clarification when required, can help ensure that our messages are received accurately and prevent miscommunication from escalating into conflict.

When miscommunication does occur, it is essential to approach the situation with humility and a willingness to accept responsibility for our part in the misunderstanding.

By acknowledging our blunders and apologizing, if necessary, we can repair trust and strengthen our relationships with others.

HANDLING CONFLICT WITH COMPASSION AND EMPATHY

Conflict is a natural part of any relationship, and how we manage it can either strengthen or diminish our connections with others. When conflicts arise, it is essential to approach them with compassion and empathy, striving to comprehend the underlying emotions and motivations driving the conflict.

One effective approach to managing conflict is through active listening and empathetic communication. This involves allowing each individual to express their thoughts and feelings without interruption, validating their emotions, and seeking to find common ground and solutions together.

It is also crucial to approach conflict with a willingness to compromise and find win-win solutions that meet the requirements of all parties involved.

This requires flexibility, receptivity, and a commitment to resolving differences peacefully.

Additionally, exercising forgiveness and letting go of resentments can help restore and strengthen relationships in the aftermath of conflict. By acknowledging our own vulnerabilities and imperfections and extending grace to others, we can create space for healing and reconciliation to occur.

REPAIRING AND STRENGTHENING RELATIONSHIPS THROUGH ADVERSITY

Adversity is an inevitable part of life, and how we navigate through challenges can profoundly impact our relationships. During difficult circumstances, it is essential to rely on each other for support and to approach adversity as an opportunity for growth and learning.

One essential strategy for repairing and strengthening relationships through adversity is through effective communication and collaboration. By openly discussing our feelings and concerns, seeking support from each other, and working together to find solutions, we can withstand the cyclones of life more effectively and emerge stronger as a result.

Additionally, exercising empathy and compassion towards ourselves and others can help us navigate through adversity with grace and resilience. By acknowledging our own vulnerabilities and struggles, and extending empathy and understanding to others, we can create a supportive and nurturing environment for healing and growth.

Finally, it is essential to focus on the positives and celebrate small victories along the road. By acknowledging and expressing gratitude for the strengths and resilience of our relationships, we can cultivate a sense of optimism and hope even in the face of adversity.

In conclusion, overcoming challenges and obstacles in relationship building requires empathy, compassion, and effective communication. By addressing miscommunication and misunderstandings with humility and candor, resolving conflict with compassion and empathy, and repairing and strengthening relationships through adversity, we can cultivate deeper connections and stronger bonds with others.

CHAPTER SEVEN

APPLYING DEEP CONNECTION IN VARIOUS CONTEXTS

In our interconnected world, the ability to cultivate profound connections extends beyond personal relationships—it permeates every aspect of our existence, from professional interactions to community engagement. In this chapter, we investigate how to employ deep connection in various contexts, focusing on three key areas:

Professional Relationships: Colleagues, Clients, and Leaders

Personal Relationships: Friends, Family, and Romantic Partners

Community and Global Connections: Bridging Differences and Fostering Unity

PROFESSIONAL RELATIONSHIPS: COLLEAGUES, CLIENTS, AND LEADERS

In the professional sphere, deep connections play a crucial role in nurturing collaboration, trust, and innovation. Whether interacting with colleagues, clients, or executives, cultivating meaningful relationships can enhance job satisfaction, productivity, and overall success.

To establish meaningful connections in professional settings, it is essential to prioritize communication, empathy, and mutual respect. Actively listening to colleagues' perspectives, acknowledging their expertise and contributions, and expressing appreciation for their efforts can help cultivate a sense of camaraderie and collaboration.

For client relationships, demonstrating empathy and understanding can enhance trust and rapport, leading to stronger partnerships and improved outcomes. Taking the time to understand clients' needs, concerns, and objectives, and offering personalized solutions and support, can deepen the connection and create long-lasting relationships.

Similarly, cultivating profound connections with leaders involves demonstrating authenticity, integrity, and professionalism. Building trust through transparent communication, reliable performance, and ethical conduct can pave the way for meaningful collaboration and mentorship opportunities.

PERSONAL RELATIONSHIPS: FRIENDS, FAMILY, AND ROMANTIC PARTNERS

In personal relationships, profound connections form the foundation of intimacy, support, and emotional well-being. Whether with colleagues, family members, or romantic companions, nurturing these connections enriches our lives and strengthens our sense of belonging and fulfillment.

To deepen personal connections, it is crucial to prioritize quality time, open communication, and vulnerability. Making time for meaningful conversations, shared activities, and expressions of affection can foster intimacy and strengthen connections with loved ones.

Active listening and empathetic communication are also essential for establishing profound connections in personal relationships. By validating each other's feelings, respecting boundaries, and offering support and understanding, we create a safe and nurturing environment for emotional expression and growth.

Additionally, exercising forgiveness and letting go of resentments can help restore and strengthen relationships in the face of conflict or challenges. By acknowledging errors, apologizing when necessary, and extending grace and understanding to others, we cultivate trust and resilience in our relationships.

COMMUNITY AND GLOBAL CONNECTIONS: BRIDGING DIFFERENCES AND FOSTERING UNITY

In an increasingly diverse and interconnected world, profound connections across communities and cultures are essential for fostering understanding, empathy, and cooperation.

By bridging differences and nurturing unity, we can establish a more inclusive and compassionate society.

To develop profound connections in community and global contexts, it is important to approach interactions with an open mind and a willingness to learn from others. Actively searching out diverse perspectives, engaging in dialogue, and practicing cultural humility can help break down barriers and cultivate mutual understanding and respect.

Collaborative initiatives that bring together individuals from diverse backgrounds and perspectives can also foster profound connections and promote positive social change. By working together towards common objectives, we can harness the collective strength and wisdom of diverse communities to resolve shared challenges and create a more equitable and sustainable future.

Finally, embracing empathy and compassion towards others, both near and far, can inspire acts of generosity and solidarity that transcend borders and boundaries. Whether through volunteer work, advocacy efforts, or supporting global causes, our actions have the power to create cascading effects of positive change and deepen connections across communities and continents.

In conclusion, applying profound connection in various contexts involves prioritizing communication, empathy, and mutual respect, whether in professional relationships, intimate connections, or community engagement. By fostering meaningful connections with colleagues, clients, loved ones, and diverse communities, we can create a more interconnected and compassionate world where every individual is valued and supported.

CHAPTER EIGHT

CONNECTION BEYOND INDIVIDUALS

In the preceding chapters, we investigated the intricacies of human connection at the individual level, concentrating on establishing authentic relationships and comprehending the foundational aspects of interpersonal bonds. However, human connection extends beyond individual interactions, incorporating broader societal and global dimensions. In this chapter, we delve into the significance of connection beyond individuals, investigating its role in creating communities, promoting well-being, and fostering global citizenship.

I. BUILDING CONNECTION IN COMMUNITIES AND SOCIETIES

Communities serve as crucibles of human connection, providing individuals with a sense of belonging, identity, and support. Whether it's a neighborhood, workplace, religious congregation, or cultural organization, communities play a vital role in shaping our social networks and collective experiences.

Building connection within communities involves nurturing a sense of inclusivity, shared purpose, and mutual support. It requires cultivating spaces for meaningful interaction, collaboration, and collective action. This can be accomplished through various initiatives, such as community events, volunteer programs, and grassroots movements that bring people together around common interests and values.

Moreover, connection within communities enhances social cohesion and resilience, enabling individuals to navigate challenges, contend with adversity, and flourish collectively. It fosters a sense of solidarity and empathy, bridging divides and nurturing understanding across diverse backgrounds and perspectives.

II. THE ROLE OF CONNECTION IN WELL-BEING AND MENTAL HEALTH

The link between human connection and well-being is well-established, with numerous studies highlighting the profound impact of social relationships on mental, emotional, and physical health. Strong social connections have been associated with reduced rates of melancholy, anxiety, and stress, as well as increased resilience and longevity.

Connection functions as a buffer against loneliness, isolation, and alienation, providing individuals with emotional support, validation, and companionship. It fosters a sense of belonging and significance, affirming one's identity and worth within social networks.

Furthermore, meaningful connections contribute to emotional regulation and self-esteem, providing individuals with a sense of security and acceptance that promotes psychological flourishing. They offer opportunities for self-expression, intimacy, and personal development, enriching individuals' lives and enhancing their overall well-being.

Conversely, social isolation and disconnection have been linked to a range of negative health outcomes, including increased risk of mental illness, cardiovascular disease, and mortality. Thus, prioritizing connection in our lives is essential for promoting holistic well-being and resilience in the face of life's challenges.

III. CONNECTION AND GLOBAL CITIZENSHIP

In an increasingly interconnected world, cultivating a sense of connection at the global level is essential for addressing pressing challenges and promoting collective well-being. Global citizenship incorporates a sense of responsibility, empathy, and solidarity towards all members of the global community, transcending national borders and cultural divides.

Connection at the global level involves recognizing our interconnectedness and interdependence as inhabitants of a shared planet. It requires cultivating empathy and understanding for diverse cultures, perspectives, and lived experiences, nurturing a sense of common humanity that transcends geopolitical differences.

Furthermore, global connection entails active engagement in efforts to promote social justice, environmental sustainability, and human rights on a global scale. It involves advocating for equitable access to resources, opportunities, and fundamental rights for all individuals, regardless of nationality or heritage.

By fostering global connection, we can leverage the collective power of humanity to resolve urgent global challenges, such as climate change, poverty, and inequality. It requires collaborative action, cross-cultural dialogue, and solidarity across borders, paving the way for a more just, equitable, and sustainable world for future generations.

In this chapter, we have investigated the significance of connection beyond individuals, concentrating on its role in building communities, promoting well-being, and fostering global citizenship. By recognizing and cultivating connection at these broader levels, we can create a more interconnected, compassionate, and resilient world for all.

CONCLUSION

EMBRACING THE JOURNEY OF DEEP CONNECTION

As we reach the culmination of our exploration into the intricacies of human connection, it is time to reflect on the profound insights gained and lessons learned along the way. Throughout this voyage, we have probed into the essence of deep connection, uncovering its transformative power and the profound impact it has on our lives and the world around us. In this concluding chapter, we will revisit key themes and contemplate the ongoing pursuit for profound connection, as well as our role in inspiring a culture of understanding and empathy in a divided world.

REFLECTING ON THE JOURNEY: INSIGHTS GAINED AND LESSONS LEARNED

Our journey into the realm of profound connection has been one of discovery, development, and self-reflection. Along the way, we have gained valuable insights into the significance of authenticity, vulnerability, and empathy in cultivating meaningful relationships. We have learned that profound connections are forged through open communication, active listening, and mutual respect, and that they require perseverance, effort, and commitment to cultivate and sustain.

We have also come to comprehend the significance of trust, forgiveness, and resilience in overcoming challenges and obstacles in our relationships. Through moments of conflict and adversity, we have learned that it is through compassion, understanding, and a willingness to embrace vulnerability that we can repair and strengthen our connections with others.

Moreover, our voyage has highlighted the interconnectedness of all human beings and the universal longing for belonging and acceptance. We have recognized the importance of diversity, inclusion, and cultural humility in bridging differences and fostering unity across communities and continents. And we have witnessed firsthand the transformative force of empathy and compassion in creating a more just, equitable, and compassionate world.

As we reflect on the insights gained and lessons learned from our voyage, we are reminded that the quest for profound connection is an ongoing process—one that requires lifelong dedication, self-awareness, and growth. It is a journey of self-discovery and self-compassion, as we learn to cultivate deeper connections with ourselves and others.

To continue our pursuit for deep connection, we must remain committed to exercising empathy, vulnerability, and authenticity in our interactions with others. We must prioritize open communication, active listening, and mutual respect in our relationships, and be willing to embrace discomfort and uncertainty as opportunities for development and learning.

Moreover, we must cultivate a mindset of inquiry and openness, searching out diverse perspectives and experiences that challenge our assumptions and broaden our understanding of the world. We must remain humble and receptive to feedback, recognizing that true development and transformation occur when we step outside our comfort zones and embrace new ways of thinking and being.

Ultimately, the pursuit for profound connection is not a destination to be attained but a voyage to be embraced—a journey of self-discovery, development, and transformation that unfolds over a lifetime. It is a journey that requires fortitude, vulnerability, and resilience, but one that is richly rewarding and profoundly meaningful.

INSPIRING A CULTURE OF UNDERSTANDING AND EMPATHY IN A DIVIDED WORLD

As we embark on the next chapter of our voyage, we are tasked to inspire a culture of understanding and empathy in a world that is increasingly divided and polarized. We are told to be beacons of light and agents of change, challenging injustice and inequality, and advocating for compassion, empathy, and inclusivity in all aspects of society.

To inspire a culture of understanding and empathy, we must lead by example, embodying the values of authenticity, vulnerability, and compassion in our interactions with others. We must endeavor to develop bridges across divides, fostering dialogue and collaboration among individuals and communities with diverse perspectives and experiences.

Moreover, we must use our voices and platforms to amplify the voices of those who are marginalized and oppressed, advocating for justice, equity, and human rights for all. We must challenge prejudice, discrimination, and hate speech wherever we encounter it, and work towards creating a world where every individual is valued, respected, and treated with dignity and compassion.

In conclusion, our voyage into the realm of deep connection has been a profound and transformative one— one that has challenged us to develop, to learn, and to evolve as individuals and as a society. As we continue our pursuit for profound connection, let us remain committed to fostering meaningful relationships, embracing diversity and inclusion, and inspiring a culture of understanding and empathy in a divided world. Together, let us work towards constructing a world where every individual feels seen, heard, and valued—a world where profound connection thrives and humanity flourishes.